# I Went Walking

**Acknowledgments**

*I Went Walking.* Text copyright © 1989 by Sue Williams. Illustrations copyright © 1989 by Julie Vivas. Reprinted by permission of Harcourt Inc.

Photography
**33,34,35,36,37,38** (girl) © 1999 Robert Kaufman  **33** (cherries)  **38** (cherry) (kiwi) Artville  **38** (orange) (banana) images Copyright © 2000 PhotoDisc, Inc.

Houghton Mifflin Edition, 2005
Copyright © 2001 by Houghton Mifflin Company. All rights reserved.

PRINTED IN CHINA

ISBN: 978-0-618-03637-0

ISBN: 0-618-03637-7

14 15-SDP-09 08 07

# I Went Walking

WRITTEN BY
## Sue Williams

ILLUSTRATED BY
## Julie Vivas

HOUGHTON MIFFLIN   BOSTON · MORRIS PLAINS, NJ

California · Colorado · Georgia · Illinois · New Jersey · Texas

# I went walking.

# What did you see?

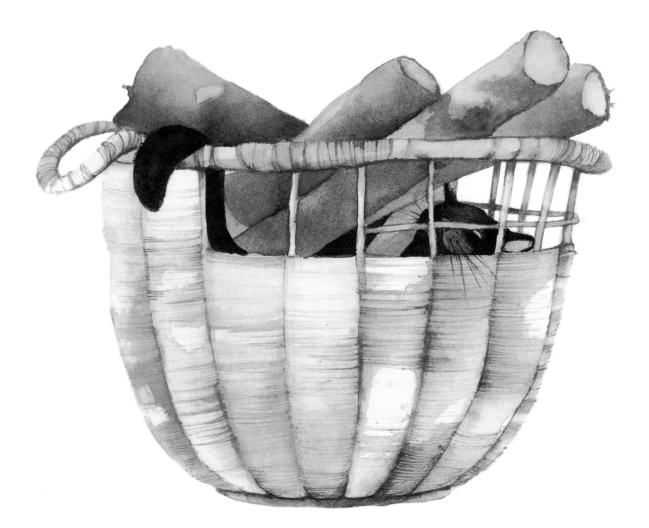

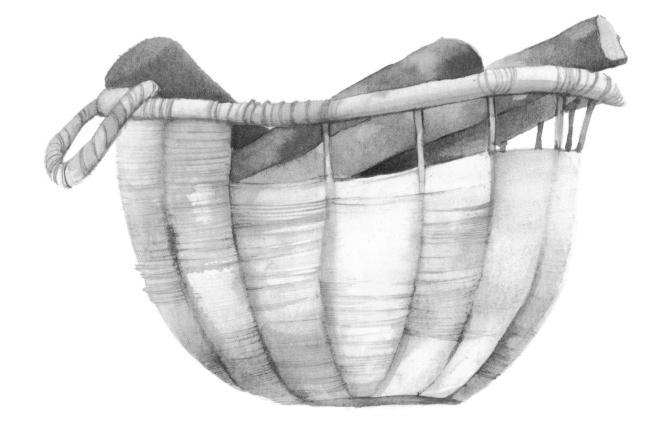

I saw a black cat
looking at me.

I went walking.

6

# What did you see?

# I saw a brown horse looking at me.

# I went walking.

# What did you see?

I saw a red cow
looking at me.

# I went walking.

# What did you see?

I saw a green duck
looking at me.

# I went walking.

# What did you see?

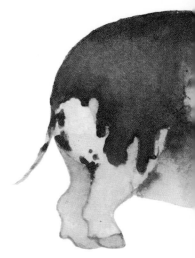

I saw a pink pig
looking at me.

I went walking.

# What did you see?

I saw a yellow dog
looking at me.

# I went walking.

# What did you see?

I saw a lot of animals
following me!

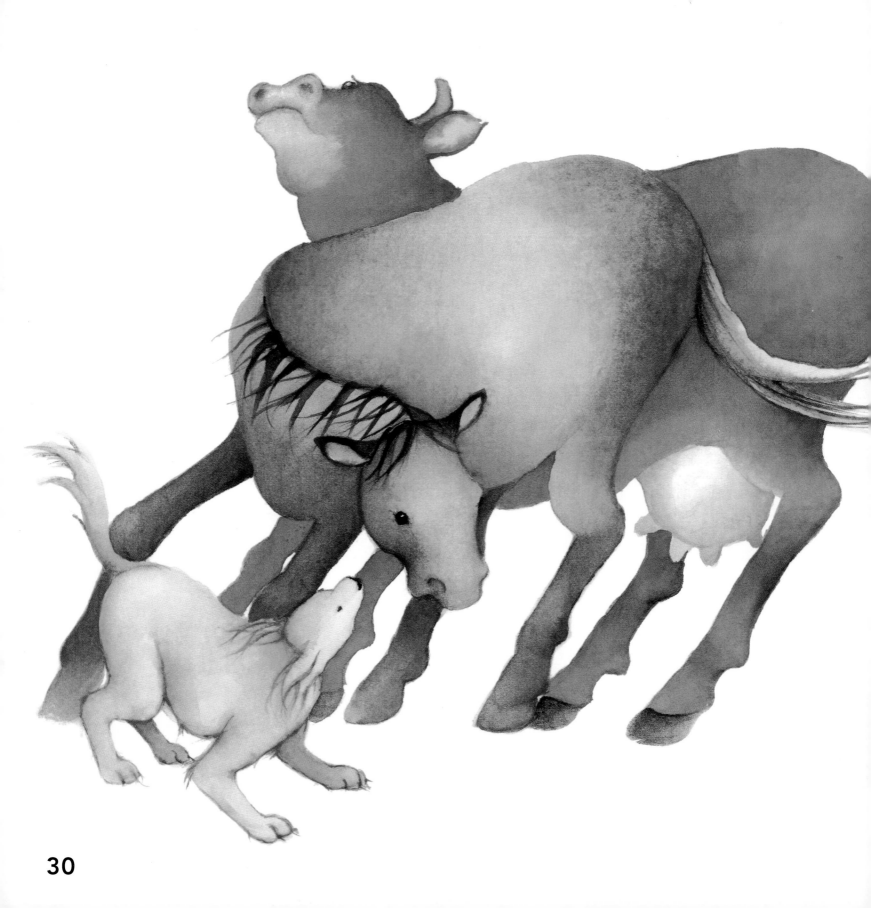

# What's My Favorite Color?

These bananas are yellow.
I like yellow, but I like green more.

These pears are green.

I like green, but I like orange more.

These oranges are orange.

I like orange, but I like red more.

These cherries are red.
Red is my favorite color because...

cherries are my favorite fruit!
What color is your favorite fruit?